VISIONARY WOMEN

✦

THE MARTYRDOM OF PERPETUA

VISIONARY WOMEN

Also in this series:

FLORENCE NIGHTINGALE: LETTERS AND REFLECTIONS
Rosemary Hartill

THE TRIAL OF JOAN OF ARC
Marina Warner

Other titles in preparation

VISIONARY WOMEN

Series editor: Monica Furlong

THE MARTYRDOM
OF
PERPETUA

with an introduction and commentary by

SARA MAITLAND

ARTHUR JAMES

EVESHAM

First published in Great Britain in 1996 by

ARTHUR JAMES LTD
4 Broadway Road
Evesham
Worcestershire WR11 6BH

ISBN 0 85305 352 9

Typeset in Monotype Sabon by
Strathmore Publishing Services, London N7

Printed and bound in Great Britain by
Guernsey Press Ltd, Guernsey, C.I.

Contents

Series Foreword *by Monica Furlong*   7

Introduction *by Sara Maitland*   11

The Passion of SS. Perpetua and Felicity   19

Commentary *by Sara Maitland*   37

The Sermons of St Augustine
    upon the Feast of SS. Perpetua and Felicity   49

Notes   61

Series Foreword

Women, in our view, have always had interesting and valuable things to say about religious meaning, and about the life of the spirit, often with a different emphasis and accent from men writing and speaking about the same thing. It is not, probably, that women are so very unlike men. It is more that, historically, their life experience has been so different that, as you might expect, they saw events and ideas through a very different glass.

In the case of Christianity it is very difficult to know what they *did* see and feel. For the first eleven centuries of the Christian church they were almost completely silent, so far as writing and public speaking were concerned, forced to be so partly by lack of education, partly by those deadly chapters in the Epistles that commanded women to be 'silent in the churches', a prohibition that extended beyond the church in a framework that set up rigid conventions, confining women within home or convent. Very, very occasionally a woman's voice breaks through – as Perpetua tells us of the horror of her imprisonment before her martyrdom (third century), or the nun Egeria tells us of her travels (fourth century). It was only from the twelfth century onwards that voices of Christian women began, very tentatively, to emerge, or at least this was the time when women's writings began to be preserved so that they have come down to us.

Nor were other religions so very different. In widely

different cultures and religions – Judaism, Buddhism, Hinduism, Islam – it was assumed, as it was in Christianity, that caring for their husbands and bearing children somehow removed women from making any other sense of their lives or of the world about them. Of course women tried to do it – how can any human being not? – but their views were not sought or recorded.

As a Christian I cannot speak for other religions (though I hope others will speak for some of them in the course of the series), but I observe that everywhere women seem less and less willing to be silent and passive participants. Within Christianity now, there is a healthy and growing remorse for all that was lost when women's voices were silenced.

This series of books attempts to salvage some of the texts (often very little known even by feminists) which remind us what it sounded like when women first began to make their voices heard, and what they said as they described the experiences which shaped their thinking. It also uses material by later women who, one way or another, broke new ground in their actions, their ideas and their self-expression. Some of these are well known, but have often been presented to us in oddly distorted ways, which suggests that it is time for some reassessments.

It is not our intention to use these texts wholly uncritically – that would be to patronize the writers – but rather to use them to develop our own thinking. The early material, in particular, often needs effort, as it invites us to make use of ideas, and a view of religion, extraordinarily different from our own.

Our hope is that readers will want to make a small

collection or library of these precious texts – a reparation to the forgotten women, but also, we believe, a fruitful source of inspiration and ideas for ourselves, the fortunate heirs of their courage and determination.

MONICA FURLONG

Introduction

In 1668 an early Christian text was included for the first time in the *Acta Sanctorum* – the Deeds of the Saints. It was an account of the final days and death in the arena of a North African martyr, Perpetua and her five companions: Felicity, Saturninus, Secundulus, Revocatus and Saturus. (In the text Perpetua is sometimes referred to as Vibia Perpetua: Vibia was her family name, which the Romans put before the personal name – as in Maitland Sara. Only Roman citizens, or highly placed provincial families, used sur-names, in this sense – none of Perpetua's fellow martyrs do.)

This text, in Latin, normally entitled *Passio Perpetuae et Felicitatis* (*The Passion* [meaning martyrdom not the impelling sexual desire] *of Perpetua and Felicity*) had been discovered earlier in the seventeenth century by Lukas Holsten among a collection of manuscripts originating from Monte Cassino. P. Poussines edited and published it shortly thereafter. Over two hundred years later, in 1889, a Greek version of this text was discovered in Jerusalem, and published the following year. There has been scholarly debate ever since as to which of these is the original – the present inclination is to treat the Latin text as primary and the Greek one as a translation.

But although this account had been lost, Perpetua and Felicity were well known in the church; they were among the martyrs named in the pre-Conciliar canon of the

Roman Catholic mass. Also extant are the four sermons that Augustine, a fellow North African, had preached on their feast day, and references to Perpetua's visions occur in the later writings of Tertullian. So its discovery was of particular importance: until then there had been no evidence whatsoever of the historical existence of two women whom the church had been naming almost daily; to discover so much about them, to have an insight into them as real women with real substance – factual and emotional – not only opened up a new realism in the Eucharistic Prayer itself, it also authenticated, at least by implication, other martyrs of the early church.

In addition to this the *Passion* is a truly remarkable text. The account of the martyrdom of Polycarp in *c.*155, an even older and equally detailed document of the church, was written as a letter to other congregations by Polycarp's friends after the event. Although it contains quotations from his defence speeches and pious speculations as to his state of mind, it is not a first-person account. *The Passion of Perpetua and Felicity* is, at least in part. The text consists of a sort of sandwich. There is a theological opening, followed by a very personal account of the days the group spent in prison, which is written by Perpetua herself. The other slice of the sandwich is a brief narrative of the experiences of some of the other members of the group and a detailed description of their individual, somewhat gruesome, deaths.

The authenticity of this *Passio* has never seriously been questioned by patristic authorities; this is the first-hand account, from AD 202, of the conversion, trial, spiritual life and death of a 22-year-old woman – 'nobly born, liberally educated and honorably wedded'. Given the degree of silence that surrounded women throughout history this is something astonishingly rare and precious. Perpetua may well not be the first Christian woman to have put her thoughts down on paper; she is, however, one of the first of whom we have any real knowledge. In her writings we can hear a voice too little heard. It is an extraordinary voice, one that I have been trying in various ways to listen to for about fifteen years.

Although scholars do not much debate the authenticity of the text, there is a critical question that has been repeatedly raised, and which is in itself extremely interesting. Were these martyrs orthodox or were they in fact heretics – Montanists, to be precise? Montanism was a rather successful heresy in the second and third centuries AD, particularly in Africa. It had been started by Lucius Montanus, a Phrygian from Pepuza, who was an ecstatic. He proclaimed himself as the founder of a new 'Church of the Spirit', and Montanism was in many ways analogous to the contemporary charismatic movement. However Montanism has two particular features of interest here: in the first place it was wide open to women's ministry – and later actually ordained women as priests; and in the second place Montanists did not accept that the Old and New Testaments marked the limits of revelation. They believed that contemporary spirit-filled interpretations, visions, and prophecies had the same status as those enshrined in the Canon of the Bible – this was a pressing issue at that time, as the Canon was in the process of becoming fixed.

It is hard to tell whether or not Perpetua herself was a Montanist as, in fact, she mentions no doctrine whatsoever, does not quote from the Bible and barely uses, even in the dreams, any exclusively Christian symbols or imagery at all, although it is obvious that she and the whole group placed a great deal of faith in her visions. What is clear is that the editor – the person who wrote the introduction and conclusion to Perpetua's account – had strong Montanist tendencies. Indeed there is a body of opinion which holds that the editor was in fact Tertullian himself, who finally left the Church and joined the Montanist sect in about 205 or 207. (Given that he was the man who first described women as 'the devil's gateway', it is quite curious that he should have found his spiritual home in a movement so committed to the preaching and ecstatic ministry of women.)

The point here is that in a sense all Christian feminists have to be Montanists in order to survive within Christianity. In particular we must believe that we are authorized 'in the spirit', regardless of whether the 'official' Church recognizes it; that we have a 'radical obedience' to an internally revealed truth, over and above our obedience to orthodoxy. While our charisms are not, on the whole, those of manic convulsive ecstasy, we do nonetheless claim that the biblical revelation cannot be complete because it is inevitably patriarchal, and that subsequent revelation, particularly in relation to women's ministry and interior spirituality, must be accorded an authority as high as Paul's and Matthew's.

In this sense, as well as in the senses that I shall argue out below, Perpetua and Felicity can be seen not simply as interesting and encouraging foresisters, but as profoundly satisfactory Matron Saints of Christian Feminism. By an 'historical accident', or 'providential grace', or both, depending on one's perspective, they have actually achieved what we all want to achieve. Coming at the very least from a marginal – if not an actually excluded – spiritual tradition, and one that was strongly woman-centred, they have ended up right in the heart of the church's most orthodox self-articulation – they are named in the Eucharistic Prayer of the Roman Catholic Church. Add to this the historical facts that they were both African; that they represent a remarkable class range – one nobly born and educated, literate, sophisticated, the other a slave; that they were sexually active, but no one in the text makes any references whatsoever to their husbands or the fathers of their babies. Their light shines across the centuries to us in the 1990s. They offer us both continuity and inspiration.

To turn now to the story: Vibia Perpetua and her companions were martyred under the persecution of Septimus Severus. The Roman state was essentially tolerant, even respectful, of other people's religious convictions. Unlike the Inquisition, the Empire did not much care what individuals believed personally, or even what they got up to in terms of worship and ritual. However, everyone was expected, regardless of faith, to make ritual sacrifices to the Emperor, as a sign of loyal solidarity with the system. Certain religious groups, for example Jews, when they were not engaged in insurrection, were shown a tolerance well beyond even this. Roman administration was more than latitudinarian; they had immense respect for ancient local traditions of theology and ethics. Christians, however, proved themselves remarkably obdurate and unassimilable; they were a new sect, they were implanting themselves deeply inside the Roman system – both in the capital and in the provinces; they had no ancient roots which could be admired and they were militantly evangelical. They would not allow themselves to be seen as a secret society or fraternity. And they refused, to the point of death, to make even the most minimal ritual sacrifice.

In an attempt to deal with the inconveniences that Christianity posed, the Empire came up with various schemes – the persecution of Septimus Severus did not attempt to punish Christians, but only to prevent any one becoming one: conversion was the offence, not conviction. This is why all the martyrs in this text were catechumens – trainee, pre-baptismal Christians. The normal method of dealing with convicts in this category was to send them to the arena, to be killed by trained gladiators or, as in this case, by wild animals. Thus two birds could be killed with one stone; the law could be seen to be upheld and a tasty variety could be introduced into the Circus for the delight of the populace. It turned out that Christians were usually rather unsatisfactory in this latter regard; they tended to be passive but completely unafraid and therefore provided very little entertainment.

We know all this from independent sources: the problems that Christianity generated for the State are well documented at various levels – including the fascinating letter from Pliny while he was provincial governor in Macedonia asking for advice on how to deal with the situation. The example of the martyrs was also held up by the teachings of the church even at this early date. Christians identified their martyrs very closely with Christ, and saw martyrdom (the word means witness – someone who bore witness to Christ even unto death) as a high road to heaven. In consequence of all this we do know a good deal about martyrdom – more, for example, than we know about ecclesial administration or forms of worship.

So here we have a quite specific group of catechumens, in Carthage, in 203: they are 'new' Christians; they are under the instruction of a deacon who is preparing them for baptism (and indeed does baptize them before they die). We know from the text that all the group were young, that Perpetua was twenty-two, married, a member of the nobility with a baby son whom she was still breast-feeding. Felicity and Revocatus were slaves.

If you have not already done so, I suggest you now read the *Passion* itself.

Sentences or phrases in italic are quotations from the Bible. Numbers in square brackets, e.g. [4], refer to the Notes which begin on p. 61.

The Passion of SS. Perpetua and Felicity

1. If ancient examples of faith kept, both testifying the grace of God and working the edification of man, have to this end been set out in writing, that by their reading as though by the again showing of the deeds God may be glorified and man strengthened; why should not new witnesses also be so set forth which likewise serve either end? Yea, for these things also shall at some time be ancient and necessary [1] to our sons, though in their own present time (through some reverence of antiquity presumed) they are made of but slight account. But let those take heed who judge the one power of one Holy Spirit according to the succession of times; whereas those things which are later ought for their very lateness to be thought the more eminent, according to the abundance of grace appointed for the last periods of time. For *In the last days*, saith the Lord, *I will pour forth of My Spirit upon all flesh, and their sons and their daughters shall prophesy; and upon My servants and upon My handmaids I will pour forth of my Spirit; and the young men shall see visions, and the old men shall dream dreams.* We also therefore, by whom both the prophecies and the new visions promised are received and honoured, and by whom those other wonders of the Holy Spirit are assigned unto the service [2] of the Church, to which also was sent the same Spirit administering all gifts among all men, *according as the Lord hath distributed unto each* – do of necessity both

write them and by reading celebrate them to the glory of God; that no weakness or failing of faith may presume that among those of old time only was the grace of divinity present, whether in martyrs or in revelations vouchsafed; since God ever works that which He has promised, for a witness to them that believe not and a benefit to them that believe. Wherefore we too, brethren and dear sons, *declare to you* likewise *that which we have heard and handled;* that both ye who were present may call to mind the glory of the Lord, and ye who now know by hearing may have communion with those holy martyrs, and through them with the Lord Jesus Christ, to Whom is glory and honour for ever and ever. Amen.

2. There were apprehended the young catechumens, Revocatus and Felicity his fellow-servant, Saturninus and Secundulus. With them also was Vibia Perpetua, nobly born, reared in a liberal manner, wedded honourably; having a father and mother and two brothers; one of them a catechumen likewise, and a son, a child at the breast; and she herself was about twenty-two years of age. What follows here she shall tell herself; the whole order of her martyrdom as she left it written with her own hand and in her own words.

3. When, saith she, we were yet with our sureties and my father was fain to vex me with his words and continually strove to hurt my faith because of his love: Father, said I, seest thou (for example's sake) this vessel lying, a pitcher or whatsoever it may be? [3] And he said, I see it. And I said to him, Can it be called by any other name than that which it is? And he answered, No. So can I call myself nought other than that which I am, a Christian. Then my father moved with this word came upon me to

tear out my eyes; but he vexed me only, and he departed vanquished, he and the arguments of the devil. Then because I was without my father for a few days I gave thanks unto the Lord; and I was comforted because of his absence In this same space of a few days we were baptized, and the Spirit declared to me, I must pray for nothing else after that water [4] save only endurance of the flesh. A few days after we were taken into prison, and I was much afraid because I had never known such darkness. O bitter day ! There was a great heat because of the press, there was cruel handling [5] of the soldiers. Lastly I was tormented there by care for the child. Then Tertius and Pomponius, the blessed deacons who ministered to us, obtained with money that for a few hours we should be taken forth to a better part of the prison and be refreshed. Then all of them going out from the dungeon took their pleasure; I suckled my child that was now faint with hunger. And being careful for him, I spoke to my mother and strengthened my brother and commended my son unto them. I pined because I saw they pined for my sake. Such cares I suffered for many days; and I obtained that the child should abide with me in prison; and straightway I became well, and was lightened of my labour and care for the child; and suddenly the prison was made a palace for me, so that I would sooner be there than anywhere else.

4. Then said my brother to me: Lady my sister, thou art now in high honour, even such that thou mightest ask for a vision; and it should be shown thee whether this be a passion or else a deliverance. And I, as knowing that I conversed with the Lord, for Whose sake I had suffered such things, did promise him, nothing doubting; and I

said: To-morrow I will tell thee. And I asked, and this was shown me. I beheld a ladder of bronze, marvellously great, reaching up to heaven; and it was narrow, so that not more than one might go up at one time. And in the sides of the ladder were planted all manner of things of iron. There were swords there, spears, hooks, and knives; so that if any that went up took not good heed or looked not upward, he would be torn and his flesh cling to the iron. And there was right at the ladder's foot a serpent [6] lying, marvellously great, which lay in wait for those that would go up, and frightened them that they might not go up. Now Saturus went up first (who afterwards had of his own will given up himself for our sakes, because it was he who had edified us; and when we were taken he had not been there). And he came to the ladder's head; and he turned and said: Perpetua, I await thee; but see that serpent bite thee not. And I said: It shall not hurt me, in the name of Jesus Christ. And from beneath the ladder, as though it feared me, it softly put forth its head, and as though I trod on the first step I trod on its head. And I went up, and I saw a very great space of garden, and in the midst a man sitting, white-headed, in shepherd's clothing, tall, milking his sheep; and standing around in white were many thousands. And he raised his head and beheld me and said to me: Welcome, child. And he cried to me, and from the curd he had from the milk he gave me as it were a morsel; and I took it with joined hands and ate it up; and all that stood around said, Amen. And at the sound of that word I awoke, yet eating I know not what of sweet.

And forthwith I told my brother, and we knew it should be a passion; and we began to have no hope any longer in this world.

5. A few days after, the report went abroad that we were to be tried. Also my father returned from the city spent with weariness; and he came up to me to cast down my faith, saying: Have pity, daughter, on my grey hairs; have pity on thy father, if I am worthy to be called father by thee; if with these hands I have brought thee unto this flower of youth – and I have preferred thee before all thy brothers; give me not over to the reproach of men. Look upon thy brothers; look upon thy mother and mother's sister; look upon thy son, who will not endure to live after thee. Forbear thy resolution; destroy us not all together; for none of us will speak openly among men again if thou sufferest aught. This he said fatherwise in his love, kissing my hands and grovelling at my feet; and with tears he named me, not daughter, but lady. And I was grieved for my father's case because he only would not rejoice at my passion out of all my kin; and I comforted him, saying: That shall be done at this tribunal, whatsoever God shall please; for know that we are not stablished in our own power, but in God's. And he went from me very sorrowful.

6. Another day as we were at meat we were suddenly snatched away to be tried; and we came to the forum. Therewith a report spread abroad through the parts near to the forum, and a very great multitude gathered together. We went up to the tribunal. The others being asked, confessed. So they came to me. And my father appeared there also, with my son, and would draw me from the step, saying: Sacrifice; have mercy on the child. And Hilarian the procurator – he that after the death of Minucius Timinian the proconsul had received in his room the right and power of the sword – Spare, said he,

thy father's grey hairs; spare the infancy of the boy. Make sacrifice for the Emperors' [7] prosperity. And I answered: I will not sacrifice. Then said Hilarian: Art thou a Christian ? And I answered: I am a Christian. And when my father stood by me yet to cast down my faith, he was bidden by Hilarian to be cast down and was smitten with a rod. And I sorrowed for my father's harm as though I had been smitten myself; so sorrowed I for his unhappy old age. Then Hilarian passed sentence upon us all and condemned us to the beasts; and cheerfully we went down to the dungeon. Then because my child had been wont to take suck of me and to abide with me in the prison, straightway I sent Pomponius the deacon to my father, asking for the child. But my father would not give him. And as God willed, neither is he fain to be suckled any more, nor did I take fever; that I might not be tormented by care for the child and by the pain of my breasts.

7. A few days after, while we were praying, suddenly in the midst of the prayer I uttered a word and named Dinocrates; and I was amazed because he had never come into my mind save then; and I sorrowed, remembering his fate. And straight way I knew that I was worthy, and that I ought to ask for him. And I began to pray for him long, and to groan unto the Lord. Forthwith the same night, this was shown me.

I beheld Dinocrates coming forth from a dark place, where were many others also; being both hot and thirsty, his raiment foul, his colour pale; and the wound on his face which he had when he died. This Dinocrates had been my brother in the flesh, seven years old, who being diseased with ulcers of the face had come to a horrible death, so that his death was abominated of all men. For him therefore I had made my prayer; and between him and me was a great gulf, so that either might not go to other. There was moreover, in the same place where Dinocrates was, a font full of water, having its edge higher than was the boy's stature; and Dinocrates stretched up as though to drink. I was sorry that the font had water in it, and yet for the height of the edge he might not drink.

And I awoke, and I knew that my brother was in travail. Yet I was confident I should ease his travail, and I prayed for him every day till we passed over into the camp prison. (For it was in the camp games that we were to fight; and the time was the feast of Geta Caesar.)[8] And I made supplication for him day and night with groans and tears, that he might be given me.

8. On the day when we abode in the stocks, this was shown me.

I saw that place which I had before seen, and Dinocrates clean of body, finely clothed, in comfort; and the font I had seen before, the edge of it being drawn down to the boy's navel; and he drew water thence which flowed without ceasing. And on the edge was a golden cup full of water; and Dinocrates came up and began to drink there from; which cup failed not. And being satisfied he departed away from the water and began to play as children will, joyfully.

And I awoke. Then I understood that he was translated from his pains.

9. Then a few days after, Pudens the adjutant, in whose charge the prison was, who also began to magnify us because he understood that there was much grace in us, let in many to us that both we and they in turn might be comforted. Now when the day of the games drew near,

there came in my father unto me, spent with weariness, and began to pluck out his beard and throw it on the ground and to fall upon his face cursing his years and saying such words as might move all creation. I was grieved for his unhappy old age.

10. The day before we fought, I saw in a vision that Pomponius the deacon had come hither to the door of the prison, and knocked hard upon it. And I went out to him and opened to him; he was clothed in a white robe ungirdled, having shoes curiously wrought. And he said to me: Perpetua, we await thee; come. And he took my hand, and we began to go through rugged and winding places. At last with much breathing hard we came to the amphitheatre, and he led me into the midst of the arena. And he said to me: Be not afraid; I am here with thee and labour together with thee. And he went away. And I saw much people watching closely. And because I knew that I was condemned to the beasts I marvelled that beasts were not sent out against me. And there came out against me a certain ill-favoured Egyptian with his helpers, to fight with me. also there came to me comely young men, my helpers and aiders. And I was stripped, and I became a man. And my helpers began to rub me with oil as their custom is for a contest; and over against me I saw that Egyptian wallowing in the dust. And there came forth a man of very great stature, so that he over-passed the very top of the amphitheatre, wearing a robe ungirdled, and beneath it between the two stripes over the breast a robe of purple [9] having also shoes curiously wrought in gold and silver; bearing a rod like a master of gladiators, and a green branch whereon were golden apples. And he besought silence and said: The Egyptian, if he shall

conquer this woman, shall slay her with the sword; and if she shall conquer him, she shall receive this branch. And he went away. And we came nigh to each other, and began to buffet one another. He was fain to trip up my feet, but I·with my heels smote upon his face. And I rose up into the air and began so to smite him as though I trod not the earth. But when I saw that there was yet delay, I joined my hands, setting finger against finger of them. And I caught his head, and he fell upon his face; and I trod upon his head. And the people began to shout, and my helpers began to sing. And I went up to the master of the gladiators and received the branch. And he kissed me and said to me: Daughter, peace be with thee. And I began to go with glory to the gate called the Gate of Life.

And I awoke; and I understood that I should fight, not with beasts but against the devil; but I knew that mine was the victory.

Thus far have I written this, till the day before the games; but the deed of the games themselves let him write who will.

11. And blessed Saturus too delivered this vision which he himself wrote down.

We had suffered, saith he, and we passed out of the flesh, and we began to be carried towards the east by four angels whose hand touched us not.

And we went not as though turned upwards upon our backs, but as though we went up an easy hill. And passing over the world's edge we saw a very great light; and I said to Perpetua (for she was at my side): This is that which the Lord promised us; we have received His promise. And while we were being carried by these same four angels, a great space opened before us, as it had been a pleasure garden, having rose-trees and all kinds of flowers. The height of the trees was after the manner of the cypress, and their leaves sang without ceasing. And there in the garden were four other angels, more glorious than the rest; who when they saw us gave us honour and said to the other angels: Lo, here are they, here are they: and marvelled. And the four angels who bore us set us down trembling; and we passed on foot by a broad way over a plain. There we found Jocundus and Saturninus and Artaxius who in the same persecution had suffered and had been burned alive; and Quintus, a martyr also, who in prison had departed this life; and we asked of them where were the rest. The other angels said to us: Come first, go in, and salute the Lord.

12. And we came near to a place, of which place the walls were such, they seemed built of light; and before the door of that place stood four angels who clothed us when we went in with white raiment. And we went in, and we heard as it were one voice crying *Sanctus, Sanctus, Sanctus* without any end. [10] And we saw sitting in that same place as it were a man, white-headed, having hair like snow, youthful of countenance; whose feet we saw not. And on his right hand and on his left, four elders; and behind them stood many other elders. And we went in with wonder and stood before the throne; and the four angels raised us up; and we kissed him, and with his hand he passed over our faces. [11] And the other elders said to us: Stand ye. And we stood, and gave the kiss of peace. And the elders said to us: Go ye and play. And I said to Perpetua: Thou hast that which thou desirest. And she said to me: Yea, God be thanked; so that I that was glad in the flesh am now more glad.

13. And we went out, and we saw before the doors, on the right Optatus the bishop, and on the left Aspasius the priest and teacher, being apart and sorrowful. And they cast themselves at our feet and said: Make peace between us, because ye went forth and left us thus. And we said to them: Art not thou our Father, and thou our priest, that ye should throw yourselves at our feet? And we were moved, and embraced them. And Perpetua began to talk with them in Greek; and we set them apart in the pleasure garden beneath a rose tree. And while we yet spoke with them, the angels said to them: Let these go and be refreshed; and whatsoever dissensions ye have between you, put them away from you each for each. And they made them to be confounded. And they said to Optatus: Correct thy people; for they come to thee as those that return from the games and wrangle concerning the parties there. And it seemed to us as though they would shut the gates. And we began to know many brothers there, martyrs also. And we were all sustained there with a savour inexpressible which satisfied us. Then in joy I awoke.

14. These were the glorious visions of those martyrs themselves, the most blessed Saturus and Perpetua, which they themselves wrote down. But Secundulus by an earlier end God called from this world while he was yet in prison; not without grace, that he should escape the beasts. Yet if not his soul, his flesh at least knew the sword. [12]

15. As for Felicity, she too received this grace of the Lord. For because she was now gone eight months (being indeed with child when she was taken) she was very sorrowful as the day of the games drew near, fearing lest for

this cause she should be kept back (for it is not lawful for women that are with child to be brought forth for torment) and lest she should shed her holy and innocent blood after the rest, among strangers and malefactors. Also her fellow martyrs were much afflicted lest they should leave behind them so good a friend and as it were their fellow-traveller on the road of the same hope. Wherefore with joint and united groaning they poured out their prayer to the Lord, three days before the games. Incontinently after their prayer her pains came upon her. And when by reason of the natural difficulty of the eighth month she was oppressed with her travail and made complaint, there said to her one of the servants of the keepers of the door: Thou that thus makest complaint now, what wilt thou do when thou art thrown to the beasts, which thou didst contemn when thou wouldst not sacrifice? And she answered, I myself now suffer that which I suffer, but there another shall be in me who shall suffer for me, because I am to suffer for him. So she was delivered of a daughter, whom a sister reared up to be her own daughter.

16. Since therefore the Holy Spirit has suffered, and suffering has willed, that the order of the games also should be written; though we are unworthy to finish the recounting of so great glory, yet we accomplish the will of the most holy Perpetua, nay rather her sacred trust, adding one testimony more of her own steadfastness and height of spirit. When they were being more cruelly handled by the tribune because through advice of certain most despicable men he feared lest by magic charms they might be withdrawn secretly from the prisonhouse, Perpetua answered him to his face: Why dost thou not

suffer us to take some comfort, seeing we are victims most noble, namely Caesar's, and on his feast day we are to fight? Or is it not thy glory that we should be taken out thither fatter of flesh? The tribune trembled and blushed, and gave order they should be more gently handled, granting that her brothers and the rest should come in and rest with them. Also the adjutant of the prison now believed.

17. Likewise on the day before the games, when at the last feast which they call Free [13] they made (as far as they might) not a Free Feast but a Love Feast, with like hardihood they cast these words at the people; threatening the judgment of the Lord, witnessing to the felicity of their passion, setting at nought the curiosity of those that ran together. And Saturus said: Is not to-morrow sufficient for you? Why do ye favourably behold that which ye hate? Ye are friends to-day, foes to-morrow. Yet mark our faces diligently, that ye may know us again on that day. So they began all to go away thence astonished; of whom many believed.

18. Now dawned the day of their victory, and they went forth from the prison into the amphitheatre as it were into heaven, cheerful and bright of countenance; if they trembled at all, it was for joy, not for fear. Perpetua followed behind, glorious of presence, as a true spouse of Christ and darling of God; at whose piercing look all cast down their eyes. Felicity likewise, rejoicing that she had borne a child in safety, that she might fight with the beasts, came now from blood to blood, from the midwife to the gladiator, to wash after her travail in a second baptism. And when they had been brought to the gate and were being compelled to put on, the men the dress of the

priests of Saturn, the women the dress of the priestesses of Ceres, [14] the noble Perpetua remained of like firmness to the end, and would not. [15] For she said: For this cause came we willingly unto this, that our liberty might not be obscured. For this cause have we devoted our lives, that we might do no such thing as this; this we agreed with you. Injustice acknowledged justice; the tribune suffered that they should be brought forth as they were, without more ado. Perpetua began to sing, as already treading on the Egyptian's head. Revocatus and Saturninus and Saturus threatened the people as they gazed. Then when they came into Hilarian's sight, they began to say to Hilarian, stretching forth their hands and nodding their heads: Thou judgest us, said they, and God thee. At this the people being enraged besought that they should be vexed with scourges before the line of gladiators (those namely who fought with beasts). Then truly they gave thanks because they had received somewhat of the sufferings of the Lord.

19. But He Who had said *Ask, and ye shall receive* gave to them asking that end which each had desired. For whenever they spoke together of their desire in their martyrdom, Saturninus for his part would declare that he wished to be thrown to every kind of beast, that so indeed he might wear the more glorious crown. At the beginning of the spectacle therefore himself with Revocatus first had ado with a leopard and was afterwards torn by a bear also upon a raised bridge. [16] Now Saturus detested nothing more than a bear, but was confident already he should die by one bite of a leopard. Therefore when he was being given to a boar, the gladiator instead who had bound him to the boar was torn asunder by the same beast and died

after the days of the games; nor was Saturus more than dragged. Moreover when he had been tied on the bridge to be assaulted by a bear, the bear would not come forth from its den. So Saturus was called back unharmed a second time.

20. But for the women the devil had made ready a most savage cow, prepared for this purpose against all custom; for even in this beast he would mock their sex. They were stripped therefore and made to put on nets; and so they were brought forth. The people shuddered, seeing one a tender girl, the other her breasts yet dropping from her late childbearing. So they were called back and clothed in loose robes. Perpetua was first thrown, and fell upon her loins. And when she had sat upright, her robe being rent at the side, she drew it over to cover her thigh, mindful rather of modesty than of pain. Next, looking for a pin, she likewise pinned up her dishevelled hair; for it was not meet that a martyr should suffer with hair dishevelled, lest she should seem to grieve in her glory. So she stood up; and when she saw Felicity smitten down, she went up and gave her her hand and raised her up. And both of them stood up together and (the hardness of the people being now subdued) were called back to the Gate of Life. There Perpetua being received by one named Rusticus, then a catechumen, who stood close at her side, and as now awakening from sleep (so much was she in the Spirit and in ecstasy) began first to look about her; and then (which amazed all there), When, forsooth, quoth she, are we to be thrown to the cow? And when she heard that this had been done already, she would not believe till she perceived some marks of mauling on her body and on her dress. Thereupon she called her brother to her, and that

catechumen, and spoke to them, saying: Stand fast in the faith, and love ye all one another; and be not offended because of our passion.

21. Saturus also at another gate exhorted Pudens the soldier, saying: So then indeed, as I trusted and foretold, I have felt no assault of beasts until now. And now believe with all thy heart. Behold, I go out thither and shall perish by one bite of the leopard. And forthwith at the end of the spectacle, the leopard being released, with one bite of his he was covered with so much blood that the people (in witness to his second baptism) cried out to him returning: Well washed, well washed. Truly it was well with him who had washed in this wise. Then said he to Pudens the soldier: Farewell; remember the faith and me; and let not these things trouble thee, but strengthen thee. And therewith he took from Pudens' finger a little ring, and dipping it in his wound gave it him back again for an heirloom, leaving him a pledge and memorial of his blood. [17] Then as the breath left him he was cast down with the rest in the accustomed place for his throat to be cut. And when the people besought that they should be brought forward, that when the sword pierced through their bodies their eyes might be joined thereto as witnesses to the slaughter, they rose of themselves and moved whither the people willed them, first kissing one another, that they might accomplish their martyrdom with the rites of peace. The rest not moving and in silence received the sword; Saturus much earlier gave up the ghost; for he had gone up earlier also, and now he waited for Perpetua likewise. But Perpetua, that she might have some taste of pain, was pierced between the bones and shrieked out; and when the swordsman's hand wandered still (for he

was a novice), herself set it upon her own neck. Perchance so great a woman could not else have been slain (being feared of the unclean spirit) had she not herself so willed it.

O most valiant and blessed martyrs! O truly called and elected unto the glory of Our Lord Jesus Christ! Which glory he that magnifies, honours and adores, ought to read these witnesses likewise, as being no less than the old, unto the Church's edification; that these new wonders also may testify that one and the same Holy Spirit works ever until now, and with Him God the Father Almighty, and His Son Jesus Christ Our Lord, to Whom is glory and power unending for ever and ever. Amen.

Commentary

This is an extraordinary text.

It is a text too that invites an infinite number of readings – Marie-Louise von Franz, [1] the Jungian analyst, for example, has written a most lovely extended essay interpreting Perpetua's visions according to the dream theories of Jung, and she arrives at some challenging and interesting conclusions. Augustine, to whom I shall return, read the *Passion* so differently from how I would choose to do so that I am forced to question my sanity or his capacity to hear another human being, particularly a female one. What follows here is a very personal reading, which is why I urged you to form your own impression before engaging with mine.

Before I go any further with the text I want to tell you a little about my context. I am forty-five years old; I am a white, western, upper-middle-class well-educated feminist woman (nobly born, liberally educated, and honorably wedded!). I am also a Christian: I, like Perpetua, and at exactly the same age as her (twenty-two), became a convert. Of course, becoming a Christian in a Christian-dominated society is a very different thing from becoming one when it is criminal to do so.

It is hard being a Christian feminist. Part of the difficulty is the sense of absence: we are broadly absent from the narrative of faith history, from the story of this community who called themselves Christians – Christ's folk.

Where we have been historically present we have been silenced, or, worse still, have had words written for us, invented, which is silencing of a very particular kind. Elizabeth Schüssler Fiorenza in *In Memory of Her* [2] advocates a process she calls 'reading the silences' in the attempt to establish the presence of women in early Christianity: the silences themselves must speak because there is little else.

In the 1970s I was struggling with this sense of exclusion and at the same time was writing a set of stories (fictional ones) which endeavoured to make imaginative connections between contemporary feminism and the long parade of actual women's lives from before the emergence of the women's movement in the nineteenth century. This particular group of stories tended to be blood-strewn tales of madness and badness done to and by women, in a timeless space between the boundaries of myth and history. These were described (wrongly in my opinion), as 'the texts of masochism'. [3]. I mention this because it was during this process that a respectable and supportive male theologian sent me a copy of *The Passion of Perpetua and Felicity*; and my instant and long-lasting involvement with it cannot be unrelated to my immense curiosity at that time about the relationship between freedom and pain.

In 1983 I published my first attempt to write about this text: a short story called 'Requiem' [4] and since then I have written about this text, these two women, in a surprising range of ways – both fictional and theological. [5] In 'Requiem', which is a fiction, I wrote about Perpetua thus:

Vibia Perpetua is twenty-two years old. She is nursing her first baby. When he cries her breasts respond, magically, which is both satisfying and embarrassing. When she is away from him for more than a couple of hours her breasts grow hard and heavy, even painful. When she feeds him she feels a strange tingling as the milk lets down and she watches his eager greedy loving lips suckle and she is enchanted. She loves her son, ignores her husband, respects her mother and hates her father. She is beautiful, nobly born, highly articulate and very well educated. She is used to being admired and getting her own way but despite this she is often frightened. When she is frightened she becomes more articulate than ever, protecting her fear – which she despises – with a brightness and certainty that others find convincing. If you like her you say that she has natural leadership potential. If you don't like her you say she is a bossy show-off. When she knows that the stage is set for her own martyrdom she thinks, rightly, that she is very young to die, but also, rightly, that she will look stunning in the arena. [6]

In another version, I wrote:

Perpetua keeps a journal. It is not altogether honest. She knows it will not be read until after her death, until after she has become a martyr and saint of the Church. It will be a testament of her passion; it will be read in the little congregations along the Mediterranean coast and up in Greece and in the islands, perhaps even in Jerusalem. She knows this so clearly that, although she means to be honest, she cannot avoid a certain self-consciousness, a certain reconstruction of herself so that she looks like a martyr and saint of the Church. She knows, for instance, that she did not speak to her father with quite the bold certainty, the high handed impertinence, the elegant wit that she records. She knows that when they took her son away her breasts ached and dripped and spoiled her tunic until Felicity bound them tightly with a long linen headpiece. She does not know if the child cried and whimpered through the night, his lips working plaintively for the tits he cannot find. But somehow tearful sulkiness and damp soggy patches down her front do not shape the narrative in the direction she would choose. She wants there to be some point to her sad demise, and the point will be the edification of Christians throughout the Empire who really will not be too interested in the inconveniences of sudden weaning. [7]

I quote myself, without apology, at some length, because it seems important to make clear how much this text means to me. Sometimes I feel that this amounts almost to an obsession, and in a moment of rare self-knowledge I have even acknowledged that I over-identify with Perpetua in particular, 'because we are quite alike in some ways'.

I also know that, just like Augustine, to whom I will return, I want to use these women's lives and words for my own purposes: to further my own twentieth-century agenda, my own feminist politics, my own theological understanding, and my own sense of heroism. However, unlike Augustine and, I must say, unlike a lot of classical theologies, I know I do not have the right to use another woman's experience without great care, especially one from such a different social environment. I think that a first-person narrative, and particularly this one, because Perpetua's voice is so clear and individual, requires a particular level of respect. I find this a recurrent problem with feminist history, since one of our criticisms of sexism is that it has used women for its own ends and denied their autonomy. How can we learn to hear and use the lives of women who can no longer defend their own version? It is an important question because to refuse to interpret lives from the past forces us into a dangerous historical isolation, and obliges us to reinvent the wheel each time. (I am told that goldfish have a seven-second memory. So long as the bowl is big enough for the goldfish to take eight seconds to swim round it, it will never get bored. I often feel that women's history – certainly the history of women's struggle against sexism – is continually and wilfully reduced to goldfish mnemonic levels. This allows male-biased commentators to say that this is how things have always been – and therefore, by implication, necessarily are.)

Often my engagement with this text feels like a dialogue, with me asking ridiculous questions of Perpetua. (For example, why, in her heroic dream, does she have to transform herself into a man in order to conquer her 'giant Egyptian'? Why does she fail to identify with Felicity and tell us more about her? And Perpetua, in this dialogue, asserts that this is *her* version and she has the right to tell it in her own way.) I constantly waver between a sense of respect, and a desire to use the text to understand more about the role of women in the earliest centuries of the Christian church.

Of course this problem – this desire to find women's voices from the past and read them as though they were post-enlightenment, feminist voices, with the same concerns, the same psychological, linguistic and political imperatives, the same oppression and consciousness of oppression, as I have – is a more general one, but for some reasons this text, this woman, Perpetua, has brought it into a particular, and long-lasting, focus for me.

I do not therefore, as you see, come to the writing of this commentary neutrally, objectively. The first thing I can do, and I think I have, is make this fact explicit. But, equally, I will not allow the difficulties of bias to prevent me trying to engage with it: such humility has not stopped hagiographers in the past, and if we allow it to stop us we simply leave their readings of women's lives unchallenged and dominant: this, for all sorts of reasons, would be a pity. I mentioned my interest in these two saints at a dinner party once, and someone asked 'Who are they?' Before I could answer, another diner, a usually sensitive and definitely anti-sexist man, said with complete innocent conviction, 'Two miraculous virgin martyrs, along with Lucy and Agnes.' (They appear with Lucy and Agnes, both definitely virginal and miraculous and probably invented, in the Roman Missal.)

Now one of the interesting things about *The Passion of Perpetua and Felicity* is not simply that neither of these two are virgins – it is that they very specifically are not: that is to say, the results of their non-virginity are part of the structure of the narrative. Perpetua's lactation is used by her father and other authorities as one means of trying to persuade her to sacrifice. Felicity's pregnancy actually does create a problem, since pregnant women could not be sent to the arena (the Empire was suffering from a worrying decline in population size, and pregnancy was treated with unusual respect at this period). [8] After some discussion, the group decide that they will pray up a premature labour for her – despite the pain and danger of such a course. No one thinks that this is unwomanly (or if they do they don't say so). Maternal virtue does not seem to count for much, but nor – here – does virginity. Later the crowd find the naked bodies of these two women, post-partum, lactating, so disturbing that they demand the games' administration give them something to wear.

But not only are they not virgins, they are also not miraculous in any sense that the medieval church would use that concept. God does not send them invisibility or shining white garments to cover their nakedness. Their attitude is very mundane: in what seems to me a very touching and authentic instance in the story, it transpires that Saturus had a bear phobia. However, when the bear, who had just torn Revocatus to pieces, was turned on Saturus, it lurked in its den and refused to fight – he was cleanly and swiftly despatched by a leopard. Any later Christian writer would have made a great deal of this divine and merciful intervention – at least an angel, and probably a prior encounter with this bear's mother, would have been introduced, and the virtue of Saturus and the slightly slap-stick hand of God would have been celebrated. This account has very little interest in the interventionist elements, but is focused on the courage and faith of these very normal human beings.

So the person who called them 'miraculous virgins' was very much mistaken. The mistake however is a natural one; unless we engage with and use these stories, the idea that all holy women are virgins merely panders to the sexist desire that they should be. This is particularly important because, as I have mentioned already, in one of her dream-visions Perpetua perceives herself as changing gender; it is very easy to see this as a 'defeat' for women. It is as men, or like men, that we must enter heaven: but the stress on the physicality of Perpetua's female-ness reduces this emphasis and represents her dream persona as just that – one of the things one's mind does do to one in dreams.

One of the things that is important about this text is a quality that it has of gender equality, which is not sexual denial. Perpetua has a spiritual authority within the group that is unquestioned. Her female-ness is not suppressed, but nor is it specially interesting, or in any way worthy of comment.

The sermons of Augustine of Hippo make a very interesting comparison on this point: and for this reason they have been included as an appendix here. Augustine lived from 354 to 430. These sermons must have been given after he was ordained in 391. Like Perpetua and Felicity, he came from Northern Africa – and, although he was educated in Italy, his ministry was exercised there. However, the ecclesial scene had changed entirely in the intervening two hundred years: Augustine was not merely a highly educated, and complex, sensitive intellectual, he was also a Bishop wielding considerable authority. Interestingly he invited the civil powers in to deal with his particular brand of antagonistic heretics, the Donatists. [9]. Augustine (like me) was not obliged to confront martyrdom: on the contrary he could and did call for the judicial punishment of other Christians. The point about these sermons is that they reveal just how much the church changed between 200 and 400 in relation to its understanding of women and their ministry. Apart from other factors, Augustine is obsessed by gender – by the merits and deficiencies of women, and by a series of gender stereotypes that at times, as I said before, make me wonder if he was capable of reading the text. (In fact, in the fourth sermon, he makes a number of factual errors that suggest he was not fully aware when Perpetua was recounting dreams rather than realities.) It is worth remembering that for twelve centuries the church had Augustine's sermons but not the original *Passion* which informed them. It is very clear that Augustine did honestly love these saints and draw inspiration from their life and witness; but the principal emotion of the *Passio* is a joyful admiration of the power of these martyrs, whereas his is gratitude to the God who can enable *even* women to behave in this courageous way. Or, as he himself put it:

> ... where the sex was more frail, there is the crown more glorious. Truly towards these women a manly courage did work a marvel, when beneath so great a burden their womanly weakness failed not. Well was it for them that they clove unto one husband, even Him unto Whom the Church, being one, is presented as a chaste virgin. ... [How proper] that women should make to fall that enemy who by a woman did make a man to fall. ... He made these women to die in manly and faithful fashion. [10]

And later:

> ... these holy and valiant ones were not only of female kind but were very women. And the one was a mother likewise, that unto the frailty of that sex might be added a more importunate love; so that the Enemy assailing them at all points and hoping they should not bear the bitter and heavy

burden of persecution, might think they should straightway yield themselves up to him and be soon his own. But they with the prudent and valiant strength of the inward man did blunt his devices every one and break his assault. [11]

It is, in a depressing way, extremely educational to read the *Passion* and Augustine's sermons together. (Though it is important to remember that Augustine was not inventing this gender obsession, nor any more guilty of it than most of his contemporaries.) He sees a specific gender meaning – and one that widens the gulf between men and women – in, for example, Felicity's labour:

As for Felicity, she was with child in her very dungeon; and in her labour did witness unto her woman's lot with a woman's cry. She suffered the pain of Eve, but she tasted the grace of Mary. A woman's debt was required of her, but He succoured her Whom a Virgin bore. [12]

Whereas the original text offers us (and presumably offered Augustine) something far more straightforward:

Because she was now gone eight months she [Felicity] was very sorrowful as the day of the games drew near, fearing lest for this cause she should be kept back ... and lest she should shed her holy and innocent blood after the rest, among strangers and malefactors. Also her fellow martyrs were much afflicted lest they should leave behind them so good a friend and as it were their fellow-traveller on the road of the same hope. Wherefore with joint and united groaning they poured out their prayer to the Lord, three days before the games. Incontinently after their prayer her pains came upon her. [13]

This businesslike attitude in relation to gender, and the authority that Perpetua has clearly been granted, do all suggest that the early church took a very different attitude to women before Christianity became the official religion of the Empire than it did thereafter. This cannot fail but be a source of authorization and inspiration to us as contemporary women.

I am arguing that *The Passion of Perpetua and Felicity* is a document of the greatest importance to contemporary women. It gives us an intimate, inside view into the mind of a woman in the third century. Although, as I have said, we have to be very careful how we hear this voice, and even more careful how we use what we hear, this does not detract from its importance – certainly it is a counter-weight to the ponderous sexism of Paul, Augustine, Jerome or Tertullian. In this regard it is worth remembering that what is in effect Perpetua's journal was cherished and preserved and considered worthy of an immediate editorial reconstruction, so that we do not just have the words but have a context which strongly suggests she was not some deviant and despised freak, but her life and death were of concern to a wider community.

Beyond this it also gives us a possible optimistic outcome of our own engagement with the church: Christianity can accommodate and incorporate the dissident voices of women; it can come to terms with women's sexual activity and theological and ministerial competence. It can even treat those things as holy.

And, finally, this very short document introduces us to two delightful lively women, who use their understanding of God to resist both their biological fathers and the patriarchal structures of law, custom and domination of their own time.

'For this reason,' says Perpetua, in the arena, facing death and still insisting that she and her friends should not have to wear idiotic and insulting fancy dress, 'For this cause came we willingly unto this – so that our liberty might not be obscured. For this cause [the cause of freedom], we have devoted our lives.' [14]

I hope Perpetua and Felicity are praying for us in heaven that we may do as bravely and as well.

SARA MAITLAND

The Sermons of St Augustine upon the Feast of SS. Perpetua and Felicity

I

Today with its anniversary and return calleth into our mind, and in a manner setteth anew before us, that day whereon the blessed servants of God, Perpetua and Felicity, being adorned with the crowns of martyrdom, did achieve the flower of perpetual felicity; bearing in the battle the name of Christ, and in the prize of battle finding their own. Their exhortations in the heavenly visions, and the triumphs of their passion, we heard when they were read to us; and all these, set out and made clear with the light of words, we have received with our ears, pondered with our minds, honoured with ceremonies of religion, praised with charity. Yet unto so holy a celebration we are bound to give also a solemn homily; and if I that speak it may not set forth their worthiness as I would, yet I bring a ready affection to the joys of so great a feast. For what thing might there be more glorious than these women, whom men may wonder at sooner than they may imitate? But this is chiefly the glory of Him, in Whom they that believe, and they that with holy zeal in His name do content one with another, are indeed *according to the inward man neither male nor female*; so that even in them that are women in body the manliness of their soul hideth the sex of their flesh, and we may scarce think of that in their bodily condition which they suffered not to appear in their deeds. The dragon therefore was trodden down by the chaste foot and victorious tread of the blessed Perpetua, when that upward ladder was shown her whereby she should go to God; and the head of the ancient serpent, which to her that fell was a stone of stumbling, was made a step unto her that rose.

What sight may be a more sweet than this, what strife a more valiant than this, what victory a more glorious than this? When their holy bodies were cast to the beasts, throughout the amphitheatre *the heathen did rage and the peoples imagine vain things. But He that dwelleth in Heaven did mock them, and the Lord laughed them to scorn.* The children of them whose voices in evil wise raged against the martyrs' flesh do with godly voices now praise the martyrs' worth; nor was the theatre of cruelty then so filled with them that gathered together unto their slaughter as is the church of godliness now with them that gather together unto their honour. Every year doth charity with religion behold that which on one day wickedness with sacrilege did commit. They also beheld, but truly not with the like intent. They with their cries did that which the beasts with their biting left yet undone. As for us, we pity the deeds of the unholy and reverence the sufferings of the holy. They saw with the eyes of the flesh that wherewith they might assuage the lust of their hearts; we with the eyes of our heart see that which was hidden from them that they might not see it. They rejoiced over the martyrs for the death of their bodies; we sorrow over themselves for the death of their souls. They without the light of faith thought the martyrs to be slain; we with the strong gaze of faith do behold them crowned.

Lastly, their insulting hath become our exulting: but this is holy and everlasting; that was unholy then, and now is nothing.

And for the prizes of martyrs, most beloved, we believe them to be the chiefest of all; and rightly do we believe it. Yet if we diligently consider their strife, we shall marvel not at the greatness of the prize. For although this life be toilsome and fleeting both, yet is there so great a sweetness in it that albeit men cannot bring it about that they shall not die, nevertheless they strive much and greatly that they shall not quickly die. For to banish death nothing may be done, but to delay death something may be done. Truly unto every soul toil is wearisome; nevertheless even they that look for nothing after this life, whether good or evil, do toil in all manner of ways unto this intent, namely that all their toil be not ended with death. And they that in error dream of false and carnal delights after death, and they that with a true faith expect repose and an unspeakable and blessed rest – do not they also busy themselves with this and with huge cares endeavour this, that they shall not quickly die? What mean so many labours for the necessity of food, such enslavement with medicines or other charges (either such as the sick demand or such as is given to them) save that they may not quickly come to that end of death? At what price then shall be purchased that freedom from death in the life to come, when but the delay thereof in this life hath so great esteem? For such strange sweetness is in this toilsome life, such is the dread of death in the nature of all that live, howsoever they live, that not even those are content to die who pass through death to the life wherein they may not die.

This joy of living, this fear of dying, the martyrs of

Christ with a pure charity, with a certain hope, with a faith unfeigned do by their eminent virtue contemn. In the strength of these they forsake the threats and the promises of the world, they *press forward to the things before*. These trample upon the serpent's head and heed not the manifold hisses of its mouth, but rather rise up thereon. For he hath the victory over all desires who subdueth the tyrannical love of this life whereof all desires are the servants: nor is a man held by any bond of this life who is not held by the love of life itself. And to the fear of death the pains of the body are wont in some wise to be compared. For sometimes the one, sometimes the other conquereth in a man. A man tormented doth lie that he may not die; another condemned to death doth lie lest he be tormented. Another speaketh the truth, not because he can bear torment but lest he be tormented if he lie to save himself. But let either fear soever conquer in any soul soever. The martyrs of Christ, for the name and the justice of Christ, won twofold victory; they feared neither to die nor to suffer pain. He conquered in them Who lived in them; so that they that lived not unto themselves but unto Him, in death itself died not. He showed them His spiritual delights that they might not feel bodily woes; in such measure as should suffice not for their failing but for their trial. In what place was Perpetua, when she felt not the battle against the maddened cow, when she asked when that should be done which had been done already? In what place was she? What saw she, that she saw not that? What tasted she, that she felt not that? With what love was she frenzied, rapt with what sight, drunk with what cup? Nevertheless she clove still to the bonds of the flesh, she had yet dying members, she was burdened yet with a corruptible body. What then, when freed from those bonds and after the pains of that deadly trial the souls of the martyrs were received and refreshed with the triumphs of angels; when it was said to them not: Fulfil that which I have commanded; but: Receive that which I have promised? With what joy now do they taste the spiritual banquet? How rest they in the Lord, in how heavenly a glory they rejoice, what man with earthly example may express?

And that life of the blessed martyrs now, though it passeth already all happiness and delights of this world, is yet but a little part of the promise, yea rather a solace of delay. But the day of recompense shall come when every body shall be restored and the whole man shall receive that which he deserveth; when the limbs of the rich man which once were adorned with a temporal purple shall be tormented with fire everlasting, and the flesh of the poor man that was full of sores shall be changed and shine out amidst the angels; albeit now also the one in hell thirsteth for a drop of water from the poor man's fingers, and the other in the bosom of the just sweetly reposeth. For even as there is great difference between the joys and sorrows of those that sleep and of those that wake, so also is there great difference between the delights and torments of men that are dead and of men that rise again; not that the spirits of the dead, as of the sleeping, must needs be deceived, but because the rest of unbodied souls is one, another their glory with heavenly bodies and the felicity of the angels, to whom shall be equalled the host of the faithful that rise again; among whom the most glorious martyrs shall shine forth with the eminent light of their proper honour, and the same bodies wherein they suffered unworthy torments shall become worthy adornments unto them.

Wherefore, as now we do, let us keep their solemnities with all devotion, with a sober joyfulness, with a holy assembly, with a faithful memory, with believing praise. It is no small part of imitation to rejoice in the virtues of them that are better than we. They are great and we little, but *the Lord hath blessed the little together with the great.* They have gone before us, they have shone out before us. If we may not follow them in deeds, let us follow them in affection; if not in glory, at least in gladness; if not in merits, in prayers; if not in their passion, in our compassion; if not in eminence, in communion. Let it not seem a little thing to us that we are members of the same body as these to whom we may not be likened. For *if one member suffer, all the members do suffer with it; so also when one member is* glorified, *all the members rejoice with it.* Glory be to the Head, Who careth both for the hands above and the feet below. As He gave His life for us, one for all, so did these martyrs imitate Him, and gave their lives for their brethren; and that a fruitful harvest should rise, a harvest of peoples as it were of seeds, they watered the earth with their blood. We also then are the fruits of their labour. We marvel at them, they have compassion on us. We rejoice for them, they pray for us. They strewed their bodies as men their garments when the foal that carried the Lord was led into Jerusalem; let us at the least cut down branches from the trees, plucking from the sacred Scriptures praises and hymns to bear forth unto the common joy. Yet do we all serve one Lord, follow one Master, attend one King; we are joined to one Head, journey to one Jerusalem, follow after one charity, embrace one unity.

II

These martyrs, brethren, were companions together; but above them all shineth out the name and merit of Perpetua and Felicity, the blessed handmaids of God; for where the sex was more frail, there is the crown more glorious. Truly towards these women a manly courage did work a marvel, when beneath so great a burden their womanly weakness failed not. Well was it for them that they clove unto one husband, even Him unto Whom the Church, being one, is *presented as a chaste virgin.* Well, I say, that they clove to that husband from whom they drew strength to resist the devil, that women should make to fall that enemy who by a woman did make a man to fall. He appeared in them unconquered, Who for their sakes became weak. He filled them with fortitude that He might reap them, Who that He might sow them did empty Himself. He led them unto this glory and honour Who for their sakes did listen to contumely and rebuke. He made these women to die in manly and faithful fashion Who for their sakes did mercifully vouchsafe to be born of a woman.

And it rejoiceth a godly soul to look upon such a sight as the blessed Perpetua hath told was revealed to her of herself, how she became a man and strove with the devil. Truly in that strife she also did run *towards the perfect man, to the measure of the age of the fulness of Christ.* And that ancient and subtle enemy that would leave no device untried, who once by a woman seduced a man and now felt a woman to play the man against him, did strive by a man to vanquish this woman; not without cause.

For he set not her husband before her, lest she that by heavenly thoughts already dwelt in the skies, by disdaining suspicion of fleshly love should remain the stronger; but he gave to her father the words of deceit, that the godly soul which might not be softened by the urging of pleasure, might nevertheless by the assault of filial love be broken. In which matter Saint Perpetua answered her father with such temperance that neither did she transgress the commandment which biddeth honour be paid to parents nor yielded to those deceits wherewith that so subtle [1] enemy tried her. And he, being on all sides overcome, caused that same father to be struck with a rod; that whereas she had contemned his words, she might at the least have compassion upon his stripes. And she grieved indeed at that insult upon her aged father, loving him yet to whom she consented not. For she detested the folly in him and not his nature; his infidelity, and not her own birth. Therefore with the greater glory she resisted so beloved a father when he counselled ill, whom she could not see smitten without lamentation; and therefore that sorrow took nothing away from the strength of her constancy, but rather it added somewhat to the glory of her passion. For *unto them that love God all things work together for good.*

As for Felicity, she was with child in her very dungeon; and in her labour did witness unto her woman's lot with a woman's cry. She suffered the pain of Eve, but she tasted the grace of Mary. A woman's debt was required of her, but He succoured her Whom a Virgin bore. Lastly her child was brought forth, timely in an untimely month. For God so willed it that the burden of her womb should not be eased in its rightful time, lest in its rightful time the glory of martyrdom should be delayed. God, I say, so willed it, that the babe should be born out of due season, yet so that to all that company should be given their due Felicity; lest had she been lacking, there should seem to have lacked not a companion only to the martyrs, but the prize of those same martyrs. [2] For that was the name of these two which is the reward of all. For wherefore do martyrs endure all things if not for this, that they may rejoice in perpetual felicity? The women therefore were called that unto which all were called. And therefore although there was in that contest a goodly company, with the names of these two the eternity of all is signified, the solemnity of all is sealed.

III

We keep to-day the feast of those two most holy martyrs who not only in their passion shone out with surpassing virtue but also for that great labour of their piety did seal with their names the reward of themselves and of their comrades likewise. For Perpetua and Felicity are the names of two, but the reward of all. Truly all martyrs would not toil for a while in that strife of passion and confession save that they might rejoice in perpetual felicity. Wherefore by the government of the divine providence it was needful that they should be not martyrs only, but likewise most close companions – as also they were – that they might seal a single day to their glory, and give to them that came after a common solemnity to be kept. For as by the example of their most glorious trial they exhort us unto their imitation, so they testify by their names that we shall receive an inseparable reward. Let both in turn hold it, both weave it together. We hope not for the one without the other. For the perpetual without felicity availeth not, and felicity faileth unless it be perpetual. Now concerning the names of those martyrs to whom this day is dedicate, let these few words suffice.

And for those women whose names these are – even as we heard when their passion was read, and as tradition hath delivered to us and we know, these holy and valiant ones were not only of female kind but were very women. And the one was a mother likewise, that unto the frailty of that sex might be added a more importunate love; so that the Enemy assailing them at all points and hoping they should not bear the bitter and heavy burden of persecution, might think they should straightway yield themselves up to him and be soon his own. But they with the prudent and valiant strength of the inward man did blunt his devices every one and break his assault.

In this company of surpassing glory, men also were martyrs; on that selfsame day most valiant men did suffer and overcome; yet did not they with their names commend this day unto us. And this was so, not because women were preferred before men for the worthiness wherewith they bore themselves, but because the weakness of women more marvellously did vanquish the ancient Enemy, and also the strength of men contended to win a perpetual felicity.

IV

Today shone forth in the Church two jewels, one brightness; because Perpetua and Felicity both do make one solemnity, nor may any man doubt of that felicity which possesseth a perpetual dignity. They were joined by their custody in the prison, they were joined also by grace; because there is no discord in them. Together they sing in the dungeon, together they go to meet Christ in the air; [3] together they battle against the maddened cow, together they shall enter into their everlasting country; together they suffered their martyrdom; the one suckled her child, the other was in labour. Perpetua said, when she lost her babe and gave up her suckling child: *Who shall separate us from the love of Christ?* Felicity groaned for her labour, and hasted fearlessly after her companions. And when she was freed from her groaning, what said she to Christ? *Thou hast broken my bonds in sunder; to Thee will I sacrifice the sacrifice of praise.* And the blessed David to comfort her groaning said: The Lord *give thee the desire of thine heart, and strengthen all thine intent.* O frailty! The shadows fled away, but the human estate fled not away. But He that overcame death did deliver her from the peril of childbearing and eased Perpetua from the pain of her breasts. When they climbed the steps of that ladder and trod on the neck of the dragon that lay in wait, [4] they came to the garden of the celestial meadows and found the good shepherd there who giveth his life for the sheep and seeketh the draught of milk from his flocks. For there sat there, saith she, a shepherd both young and old, fresh in years and hoary of head, who knoweth not age. Youthful was his shining countenance, because he is *ever the same, and his years shall not fail.* Hoary was his head, because in the martyrs the righteous Lord did *love righteousness* and acknowledge equity. Round about him lay his sheep reclining, and himself with a shepherd's hand did milk them in whom he found store of milk and a conscience fruitful of holiness. With his hands he milked them and spoke to them with fatherly comforts, with the heavenly promises that were prepared, saying: *Come, ye blessed of my Father, receive the kingdom which was prepared for you from the foundation of the world.* And he showed them vessels of milk brimming with a pure heart through the shining gift of alms, and said: *I was hungry, and ye gave me to eat; thirsty, and ye gave me drink.* From this sweet shepherd Perpetua received new milk ere she shed her precious blood. They answered, Amen, and began to ask for the grace of sanctity. They prayed in prison, being now at ease concerning the shepherd. Lord, said they, let not our confession of Thee be dry, that we also may be found worthy to be joined to Thy precious flocks and not to be separated from Thy martyrs. And there was set before them in vision a wrestling place, a solemn arena in the amphitheatre. There came that ill-favoured [5] Egyptian who in heaven was the comely Lucifer; being about to do battle he wallowed in the dust; and Perpetua being about to triumph in the Lord her Saviour, joined her hands together into a cross, having before her a young man sent by the Lord to defend her. She received from her victory a triumph, she won a branch from her crown. Let us also offer unto them our gifts. Others in that time offered them the visitation of their prison; let us offer to them the prayers of their solemnity, that with all saints we may be found worthy of a kingdom.

Notes

The Passion of SS. Perpetua and Felicity

[1]   Or perhaps, 'familiar'.

[2]   Literally, 'furnishing'.

[3]   In the symbolism of early Christian art such a vessel was used to signify a Christian's good works, or sometimes the Christian himself as the 'vessel of Christ' St Perpetua may have had this in mind.

[4]   The *ab aqua* of the Latin most probably means not 'from' the water of baptism, but 'after' it; for the moments just afterwards were held to be specially apt for the request of particular graces (Tert. *De Baptismo*, c. xx).

[5]   Or it may be 'extortion'.

[6]   Or 'dragon'.

[7]   These were the associated Emperors Severus and Caracalla.

[8]   Geta was the younger brother of Caracalla, and had been raised to the rank of Caesar in 198. The word *natale* here has not its strict sense of 'birthday' (for according to Spartianus, Geta was born on 27 May), but means the feast commemorating his elevation.

[9]   The interpretation of this difficult passage is probably this. The man wears a white *tunica*, purple-edged and open in front (somewhat like a white cope with purple orphreys); beneath it is a purple

undergarment, visible between the purple bands of the *tunica*.

[10] The liturgical Latin is used in the English here, for the Latin original gives the liturgical Greek: *Agios, agios, agios.*

[11] 'And God shall wipe away all tears from their eyes' (Apoc. VII, 17).

[12] The narrator's words are not clear, but seem to mean that Secundulus was beheaded in prison.

[13] At which ancient, as modern, custom allowed the condemned choice of food and drink. The martyrs used the occasion for the celebration of the *Agape*.

[14] The Roman names probably represent the Carthaginian deities Baal-Ammon and Tanit.

[15] Literally, 'that firmness (of hers), noble to the end, resisted.'

[16] See the title-page of Leclercq, *Les Martyrs*, I, for the reproduction of such a scene from a second-century lamp. The 'bridge' in the next sentence is distinct from that in this; it probably crossed the ditch or moat at the edge of the arena.

[17] The end of the soldier's story will be found by those who wish it in the entry of 29 April in the ancient calendar of the Church in Carthage: *Pudens Martyr.*

Commentary

[1] Marie-Louise von Franz, *The Passion of Perpetua* (The Jungian Classic Series, Spring Publications, 1980).

[2]   Elizabeth Schüssler Fiorenza, *In Memory of Her* (SCM Press, 1983).

[3]   The first group of these stories was published in Sara Maitland, *Telling Tales* (Journeyman Press, 1981) – along with some quite different sorts of stories – and another set in Aileen la Tourette and Sara Maitland, *Weddings and Funerals* (Brilliance Books, 1983).

[4]   la Tourette and Maitland, *Weddings and Funerals*, republished in Sara Maitland, *Women Fly When Men Aren't Watching* (Virago, 1993).

[5]   Most recently, for example, in Sara Maitland, *Angel and Me* (Mowbray, 1995).

[6]   Cf. note 4.

[7]   Maitland, *Angel and Me* (Mowbray, 1995)

[8]   Peter Brown, *Body and Society* (Faber, 1988). In this fascinating and readable book, Brown actually goes further than merely recording it: he suggests that the stress of virginity arose originally in the Church as a radical anti-state political act. In the absence of contraception the refusal by women to have sex was a refusal to act as a 'good citizen': far from being a dualist stance it could be a prophetic and political act.

[9]   It is probably worth noting that the Donatists were not gentle souls whose intellectual freedoms alone caused Augustine to intervene so determinedly. They were more than disruptive: they were extremely hard-line, often violent and given to killing people with whom they did not agree, by, for instance, tossing them off church towers.

[10] *Sermons of St Augustine*, II, p. 55 above.

[11]   *Sermons of St Augustine*, III, p. 58 above.
[12]   *Sermons of St Augustine*, II, p. 56 above.
[13]   *Passion*, ch. 15, pp. 29–30 above.
[14]   *Passion*, ch. 18, p. 32 above.

Sermons of St Augustine

[1]   Reading *astutior*, the emendation of the Maurists for MS *altior*. The Pseudo-Augustine in a parallel passage (Morin, *S. Aug. Tractatus Sive Sermones Inediti*, p. 197, l. 30) has *insidiosius agens*.

[2]   *Ipsorum martyrum praemium*. But perhaps *ipsum* should be read for *ipsorum* – 'the very prize of the martyrs'.

[3]   *Passion*, ch. 12.

[4]   *Passion*, ch. 4. But Felicity was not with Perpetua in the vision; and in much that follows the writer departs from the original narrative.

[5]   The translator supplies the adjective, which is wanting in the text but is demanded by the antithesis. In the actual vision of Perpetua (ch. 10) the words used are *Ægyptius fœdus specie*. Our author may have repeated *fœdus*, but cadence (and probably rhyme) might suggest a different word. *Lucifer speciosus* would be exactly balanced by *Ægyptius maculosus*.